629.222 F537M

D1545032

WWW.SHOREWOODLIBRARY.ORG

LIGHTNING BOLT BOOKS™

Cool Muscle Cars

Jon M. Fishman

Lerner Publications • Minneapolis

Copyright © 2019 by Lerner Publishing Group, Inc.

All rights reserved. International copyright secured. No part of this book may be reproduced, stored in a retrieval system, or transmitted in any form or by any means—electronic, mechanical, photocopying, recording, or otherwise—without the prior written permission of Lerner Publishing Group, Inc., except for the inclusion of brief quotations in an acknowledged review.

Lerner Publications Company
A division of Lerner Publishing Group, Inc.
241 First Avenue North
Minneapolis, MN 55401 USA

For reading levels and more information, look up this title at www.lernerbooks.com.

Library of Congress Cataloging-in-Publication Data

The Cataloging-in-Publication Data for *Cool Muscle Cars* is on file at the Library of Congress.
ISBN 978-1-5415-1997-8 (lib. bdg.)
ISBN 978-1-5415-2755-3 (pbk.)
ISBN 978-1-5415-2507-8 (eb pdf)

Manufactured in the United States of America
1-44333-34579-1/11/2018

Table of Contents

It's a Muscle Car!

Vroom! Vroom! A muscle car driver pushes the gas pedal. The engine roars. Smoke flows from the tires as the car speeds away.

Muscle cars are medium-sized cars. They have big engines

Sometimes carmakers build more than one model of the same type of car. The model with the more powerful engine may be a muscle car.

Some people disagree about which cars are muscle cars. But everyone agrees that muscle cars should go fast and be fun to drive!

The Muscle Car Story

People began making cars in the late nineteenth century. Right away, drivers wanted to go fast. Carmakers made cars go faster by giving them powerful engines.

Drivers loved to race their souped-up cars. NASCAR formed in 1947 to organize races. The races featured normal-looking cars with huge engines.

A souped-up car is one that has special parts, such as a giant engine.

NASCAR became a smash hit with racing fans. Carmakers wanted to cash in on NASCAR's success. By the 1960s, they sold many cars with big engines to the public.

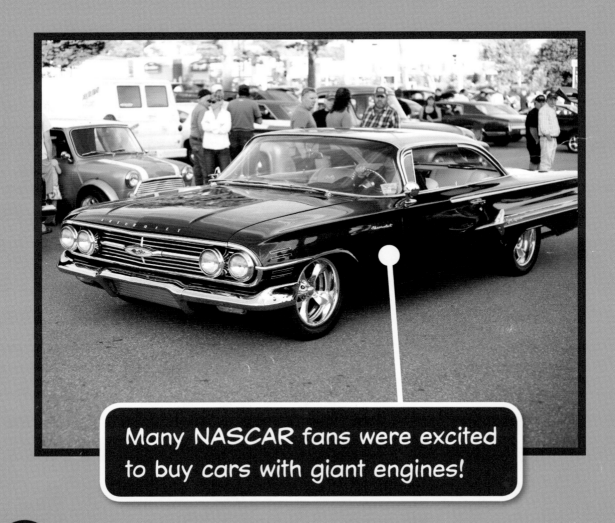

Many NASCAR fans were excited to buy cars with giant engines!

Fuel can be expensive, and fuel costs went up in the 1970s.

Powerful engines often burn a lot of fuel. Buyers wanted cars that burned less fuel beginning in the 1970s. Modern muscle cars use less fuel but still go fast.

Muscle Car Parts

A muscle car zooms down a city street. Its big engine makes a deep drumming sound. Some muscle car engines make a lot of noise.

Most muscle car engines have eight cylinders to create plenty of power. The powerful engine needs a lot of air to burn fuel. A supercharger pulls air into the engine.

This car's supercharger sticks out above the hood.

Most muscle cars have two doors. There's usually room for two to four people inside the car. Fasten your seatbelt!

This car has flames painted on the hood.

Muscle cars are built to look fast and tough. Some owners give their cars fun paint jobs.

Muscle Cars in Action

Squeak! Squeak! A muscle car owner turns a bolt in his car's engine. Many people enjoy working on muscle cars.

People work hard to make their muscle cars look and run a certain way. Then they often want to show them off! Muscle car owners take part in parades and tours.

People like to watch muscle cars in action almost as much as they like to drive them. Muscle cars appear in many movies and TV shows.

Many people know Bumblebee, the car from the Transformers movies.

Muscle cars can go from 0 to 60 miles (97 km) per hour in less than five seconds. They're faster than ever and better at saving fuel. Muscle cars will always go fast and be a blast to drive!

Muscle Car Diagram

roof

supercharger

seat

tire

Muscle Car Facts

- A website ranked the 2017 Dodge Charger as the fastest muscle car of the 2010s. It can go from 0 to 60 miles (97 km) per hour in 3.4 seconds.

- Some people consider the 1949 Oldsmobile 88 to be the first muscle car. It wasn't nearly as fast as newer cars. It took 13 seconds to go from 0 to 60 miles per hour.

- In 2014, a Ford GT40 muscle car built in 1964 sold for $7 million!

Glossary

bolt: a metal pin

cylinder: a chamber in an engine where a piston moves. Engines with more pistons usually have more power.

fuel: something that is burned to make power

gas pedal: a foot-operated lever that makes a car go faster

model: a version of a product

NASCAR: National Association for Stock Car Auto Racing

souped-up: increased in power

supercharger: a device that pushes air into an engine

Further Reading

Ducksters: NASCAR
http://www.ducksters.com/sports/nascar.php

Early Cars: Fact Sheet for Children
https://www.si.edu/spotlight/early-cars

Parrish, Margaret, ed. *Fast Cars.* Mankato, MN: New Forest, 2012.

Reinke, Beth Bence. *Race Cars on the Go.* Minneapolis: Lerner Publications, 2018.

Sandler, Michael. *Hot Hot Rods.* New York: Bearport, 2011.

Index

Photo Acknowledgments

The images in this book are used with the permission of: Darren Brode/Shutterstock.com, p. 2; nickej/iStock/Getty Images, p. 4; Grzegorz Czapski/Shutterstock.com, pp. 5, 11; sierrarat/E+/Getty Images, p. 6; itsskin/Vetta/Getty Images, p. 7; Lux Blue/Shutterstock.com, p. 8; RacingOne/ISC Archives/Getty Images, p. 9; sshaw75/iStock/Getty Images, pp. 10, 14; AM-C/E+/Getty Images, p. 12; Jeremy Warner/Shutterstock.com, p. 13; Faded Beauty/Shutterstock.com, p. 15; Monkey Business Images/Shutterstock.com, p. 16; Steve Lagreca/Shutterstock.com, p. 17; Dmitriy Bryndin/Shutterstock.com, p. 18; Lucie Lang/Shutterstock.com, p. 19; littleny/iStock/Getty Images, p. 20; betto rodrigues/Shutterstock.com, p. 22.

Front cover: benedek/iStock Unreleased/Getty Images.

Main body text set in Billy Infant regular 28/36. Typeface provided by SparkType.